CELEBRITY BIOS

Usher

Morgan Talmadge

HIGH
interest
books

Children's Press
A Division of Grolier Publishing
New York / London / Hong Kong / Sydney
Danbury, Connecticut

Book Design: Nelson Sa
Contributing Editor: Jennifer Ceaser

Photo Credits: Cover, p. 4 © The Everett Collection; pp. 7, 9 © Pacha/Corbis; p. 11 © The Everett Collection; p. 13 © Tim Mosemfelder/Corbis; p. 14 © Ethan Miller/Corbis; p. 17 © Pacha/Corbis; pp. 20, 23, 25, 27 © The Everett Collection; p. 28 © Mitch Gerber/Corbis; p. 31 © Mitch Gerber/Corbis; p. 33 © Pacha/Corbis; p. 35 © Ronnie Wright/Corbis; p. 39 © Pacha/Corbis

Library of Congress Cataloging-in-Publication Data

Talmadge, Morgan.
　Usher / by Morgan Talmadge.
　　p. cm. (Celebrity bios)
　　ISBN 0-516-23421-8 (lib. bdg.) – ISBN 0-516-23583-4 (pbk.)
　　1. Usher—Juvenile literature. 2. Singers—United States—Biography—
　　Juvenile literature.
　[1. Usher. 2. Singers. 3. Afro-Americans—Biography.] I. Title. II. Series.

ML3930.U84 T35 2000
782.421643'092—dc21
[B]

00-031672

CONTENTS

CHAPTER ONE

Young Usher

"My mother taught me . . . to be positive, and no matter how hard life gets, always look at it on the up and up because you're still living. And you're living for a reason and I found my reason."
—Usher on *MTV*

Usher is a man of many talents. His 1997 album *My Way* has sold more than 11 million copies worldwide. His 1999 live record and video together have sold more than one million copies. As an actor, Usher has appeared in several successful movies and TV series. He has won many awards for his work both as a musician and an actor. He is a generous person who gives to charity and supports young artists who are trying to break into show business. Usher also is a great role model.

Usher is a successful musician who has sold millions of records.

EARLY CHILDHOOD

On October 14, 1978, Usher Raymond IV was born in Dallas, Texas. Usher was named after his father, Usher Raymond III. Usher's parents divorced when he was just a year old. Usher moved with his mother, Jonetta Patton (known as J-Pat), to Chattanooga, Tennessee. In Chattanooga, Usher's mom remarried and Usher's little brother, James, was born.

By the time Usher was nine years old, he was singing in the church choir. Over the next two years, he entered several talent contests. At age eleven, Usher won a talent contest, beating out several older performers. Usher proudly recalled that day in *Teen People*, "I was a middle-school student and I won a high-school talent competition."

Usher's mom knew that Usher's talents could take him anywhere he wanted to go. So in 1990, she moved the family to Atlanta, Georgia, where there would be more opportunities for Usher to succeed.

Fans go wild for Usher's smile.

ON THE ROAD TO SUCCESS

In Atlanta, Usher's mom got a job as choir director at a Baptist church. Usher continued to perform at church and to compete in area talent contests. One of the people he met at a talent show was Bryan Reid, the brother of L.A. Reid, from LaFace Records. Bryan thought Usher was the kind of performer for whom L.A. Reid was looking. In 1992, fourteen-year-old Usher auditioned for LaFace Records. The record executives were excited by what they heard and immediately signed Usher to a contract with the label.

In 1993, Usher was featured on the television show "Star Search." Usher won in his category and was chosen as the show's Best Teen Male Vocalist. After winning "Star Search," Usher was asked to perform a song for the soundtrack of the movie *Poetic Justice*, which starred Janet Jackson. That song, "Call Me A Mack," was released as Usher's first single in 1993.

Usher has a unique sense of style.

THE FIRST ALBUM

In 1994, Usher started working on his first album, *Usher*, for LaFace Records. The producer of the album was Sean "Puffy" Combs, also known as Puff Daddy. Puffy brought Usher to live with him in New York City while they worked on the album. "Usher became like a little brother to me," Puffy recalled in *People*. "I got to see all of his talents. Usher's easy to work with, he listens, he's an incredible singer and an excellent dancer."

It was an honor for Usher to have his first album produced by Puff Daddy. However, the two didn't agree on everything, especially when Puffy tried to turn Usher into something that he wasn't. "It was the wrong direction, that whole bad-boy thing," Usher recalled in *People*. "Cool guys smile. Cool guys can be sexy."

There were other problems during recording. Usher turned fifteen, and puberty caused his

Usher's first album was a challenge to make.

voice to change while the album was being recorded. He told *Teen People* that his voice change was "the most tragic thing that has ever happened to me." Several voice coaches were brought in to help Usher with his singing. Usher felt, though, that the record producers had given up on him. "Instead of having support from certain people who I believed in, they turned away and just didn't believe in me," Usher painfully recalled in *Teen People*. To make matters worse, Usher began to suffer from terrible acne. "His whole face just broke out because he was so nervous," his mother J-Pat recalled in *Teen People*.

Usher struggled through his vocal problems and finally completed recording. Released in 1994, the album *Usher* yielded the single "Think of You." The single climbed into the Top Ten on the music charts. "Think of You" went gold, selling more than 500,000 copies.

Usher is a fantastic dancer and goes all out to please his fans.

Young Usher

Even with a hit single, *Usher* did not sell well enough to impress record executives. Also, Usher's producer, Puff Daddy, was too busy with his own career to offer direction to the young performer. It was a disappointing time, but Usher did not give up. There were plenty of challenges ahead. Usher still had to finish high school. He was interested in acting. And before long, he wanted to record another album.

CHAPTER TWO

Usher, the Musician

"My music will never leave me, my music will comfort me in a time of need."
—Usher in an interview with *MTV*

Although his first album was not a huge success, Usher was still in demand as a singer. He contributed to the soundtrack of the 1994 movie *Jason's Lyric*, which starred Jada Pinkett. The soundtrack featured a song called "U Will Know," performed by several male singers (including Usher) singing together as Black Men United. In 1995, singing sensation and friend Monica asked Usher to sing a duet with her on the song "Let's Straighten It Out." Usher also recorded a holiday jingle for

Usher is a talented songwriter. He cowrote six songs on *My Way*.

Coca-Cola that same year. He contributed a song to a tribute album for the 1996 Olympics. The album was called *Rhythm of the Games*. Also, with the help of a tutor, Usher finished high school.

DOING IT HIS WAY

LaFace Records had not given up on Usher, even though his first album did not sell as well as the label had hoped. In 1996, LaFace asked three of the biggest music producers—Babyface, Teddy Riley, and Jermaine Dupri—to work on Usher's new project. These producers brought their own unique styles to the recording studio, but they also listened to what seventeen-year-old Usher wanted. "What we ended up writing and recording was about my life—about what I've dealt with, being a teenager who's going into manhood," Usher told fans on his official Web site. Usher also cowrote six songs, demonstrating his skill as a songwriter.

The result was the *My Way* album which was released in 1997. Babyface produced the beautiful ballad "Bed Time." He also arranged for Monica to help out on the album by recording a new duet, "Slow Jam." Teddy Riley also produced a ballad for the album. But it was Jermaine Dupri who produced the songs that would become big hits. "You Make Me Wanna . . ." and "Nice and Slow" raced up the music charts. The single "You Make Me Wanna. . ." went platinum (selling more than one million copies) and spent fourteen weeks as number one on the Billboard R&B (rhythm and blues) and pop music charts. *My Way* became the eleventh best-selling record of 1998.

My Way established Usher as one of music's hottest young artists. He was named 1998's

Billboard Entertainer of the Year. He won a Soul Train Music Award for Best R&B/Soul Single for "You Make Me Wanna . . ." Usher also snagged a Grammy nomination for Best Male R&B Vocal Performance for the song "My Way."

USHER ON TOUR

With the success of *My Way*, Usher knew that it was time to bring his music to the fans. He worked on his dance moves with the help of a choreographer. He also shed his baby fat and created a lean and sexy new image. When Usher performed live at the Apollo Theater in September 1997, the audience went wild for the handsome and talented young performer.

In November of that year, Usher began touring to support the success of his album. He opened for Puff Daddy's No Way Out tour. After that tour wrapped up in early 1998, Usher immediately signed on as the opening act for Mary J. Blige. Then Usher opened for Janet Jackson on her Velvet Rope tour in July.

Usher is known as an incredible live performer. He spends many hours studying the moves of dancers he loves, including Michael Jackson, Fred Astaire, and Gene Kelly. "I study Gene Kelly for the grace, the shoulders, the posture," Usher told *USA Today*. Rehearsals for his tours can be exhausting and even dangerous. Usher dislocated his shoulder while rehearsing the choreography for his 1999 tour of Australia and New Zealand and had to cancel the shows.

There also have been some problems on tour. On a 1998 tour of England, a fan opened a can of tear gas in the audience before Usher even reached the stage. No one died, but a few fans had to be hospitalized because of breathing difficulties. Security also is challenging. "People have to dress up as me and be decoys," Usher told *People* about protecting his safety in large crowds.

CHAPTER THREE

Usher, the Actor

"I started off as just a full-time singer, which is basically the first love of my life. And actually acting came about just like Will Smith . . . it was an opportunity for me."
— **Usher in an *MTV* interview**

In 1997, Usher made his acting debut on the television show "Moesha," which starred Brandy Norwood. Usher played Moesha's boyfriend, Jeremy. Critics and fans were impressed with Usher's performance. Usher went on to do guest appearances on the TV series "The Parent 'Hood" and "Promised Land." Then in June 1998, Usher appeared in eight episodes of the daytime soap opera "The Bold and the Beautiful." Usher later was nominated in 1999 for an NAACP Image Award for Outstanding Actor in a Daytime

In 1997, Usher made a guest
appearance on the TV show "Moesha."

Drama Series. The NAACP is an organization that fights for racial equality. They give these awards to performers who present positive images of African Americans.

LEAP TO THE BIG SCREEN

Usher made the leap from television to movies in 1998. His first role was a high school student possessed by aliens in the science fiction thriller *The Faculty*. In 1999, he had a small role as the campus dee-jay in the movie *She's All That*, starring Rachael Leigh Cook and Freddie Prinze Jr. That same year, Usher costarred with Vanessa L. Williams in *Light It Up*. He played Lester Dewitt, one of a group of teens that tries to improve the rundown condition of their high school. Usher's friend and producer Babyface produced the movie.

By the time *Light It Up* started filming, Usher's album *My Way* was a smash hit. The producers of *Light It Up* asked Usher to record a song for the

Usher played a dee-jay in the 1999 movie *She's All That*.

movie's soundtrack. Surprisingly, Usher said no. "I wanted to be taken seriously as an actor," he recalled in *Entertainment Weekly*. Usher also had to make a difficult choice when he took on the role in *Light It Up*. Because of scheduling difficulties, he had to stop performing as the opening act for Janet Jackson's Velvet Rope tour. Yet Usher didn't regret his decision. He told the *San Francisco Chronicle*, "I'm happy that I had a chance to show myself as an actor."

CONTINUED SUCCESS

The film offers kept coming. In 1999, Usher began filming *Texas Rangers* with costars James Van Der Beek, Dylan McDermott, and Rachael Leigh Cook. The film, which came out in 2000, is about a group of young people who fight to keep the West safe after the American Civil War. Usher learned how to ride a horse during filming, which he described to MTV as pretty painful. "I got a few sores, you know,

Usher starred as Lester DeWitt in *Light It Up*.

blisters from riding on those horses. Saddles are hard when you're not used to them."

Usher also acted and sang in the TV musical "Geppetto," starring Drew Carey. His character was the singing Ring Leader on Pleasure Island. It aired on ABC's "Wonderful World of Disney" on May 7, 2000. Usher told MTV why the story appealed to him: "The Pinocchio story was something that I loved as a kid, and I thought it was really creative of Disney to do it from the father's perspective."

Usher has even written a screenplay for a movie called *Façade*. *Façade* is about artists and the lives that they lead. Usher says that it is similar to the movie *Purple Rain*. Prince starred in and created the music for *Purple Rain*. Usher told MTV, "You'll get a chance to see what entertainers go through, the good and the bad." Usher plans to star in the movie, as well as to record and produce the film's soundtrack.

Usher costarred with Elijah Wood in *The Faculty*.

CHAPTER FOUR

Family, Charity, and the Future

"Hopefully, I'll keep going in the right direction, as long as I keep my head to the sky, keep a positive attitude, and do what I love."
—Usher in an *MTV* interview

One of the things that was hard for Usher when he was a boy was that he had no father figure. His own father, Usher Raymond III, was not involved in his life after his parents broke up. As a result, Usher looked to Puff Daddy and L. A. Reid from LaFace Records for support. Usher recalled in *USA Today*, "L. A. took me under his wing like a father." When Usher saw his real father again, it was fifteen year later, at his grandmother's

Usher has become a successful young man despite not growing up with a father.

funeral. In a 1998 interview with *Teen People*, Usher explained his feelings about his father: "I don't have any remorse, because I've never had a relationship with him. How can you love somebody or hate somebody you've never known?"

When Usher was a young teenager, his mother divorced his stepfather, Terry Patton. However, Usher is very devoted to his younger half-brother, James. Usher also has a lot of support from the rest of his family. He is close to his grandparents, uncles, aunts, and cousins. However, Usher's closest relationship is with his mother. "She's always been there for me," Usher told the Associated Press. "It always helps to have someone behind you, and my mother was my person."

USHER BRANCHES OUT

Usher was able to use the support of the people closest to him to learn new things. He

Usher at the Grammy Awards.

never has been afraid to look for advice or to ask for help. "Figure out what you need and find someone to help you get there," Usher told *USA Today*. Usher first learned about singing and performing from his mother. L. A. Reid taught Usher about older music styles and performers like The Dells and The Spinners. Puffy Combs taught him about producing music.

In 1998, Usher took what he learned from his mentors and created his own record label, Us Records. One of the first artists he signed to the label was a Puerto Rican singer named Melinda Santiago. Usher is producing some of the tracks on her first album. Wyclef Jean of The Fugees may produce other tracks on Melinda's record.

Working with Melinda is just one example of the support Usher shows to other performers. Usher produces talent shows in Atlanta, where he made his home. Usher got

Usher always looks his best.

his big break on "Star Search," so he is trying to give other talented kids opportunities, too. "I'm more or less trying to do something positive for kids who live in the inner city," Usher told MTV about the talent searches. In April 1999, Usher hosted a three-day fan club convention for his fans. The convention featured a talent contest and a fashion show. The convention also featured Puff Daddy, Jermaine Dupri, and members of the Atlanta Falcons football team. Usher hopes that events like these can act as inspiration for kids who are trying to fulfill their dreams.

USHER GIVES BACK

Usher knows how fortunate he has been, and he knows it's important to portray a positive image. For this reason, Usher has involved himself in a number of activities that benefit youth and the community. "A lot of negativity comes through life for a lot of

Usher donates his basketball skills to help children's charities.

minorities," Usher explained to *Rolling Stone*. "I try to be positive and I try to act as a positive role model."

Usher participated in the NBA's Stay in School program, explaining to youths the importance of education. He was the national spokesperson for the Get Big on Safety campaign for the U.S. Department of Transportation. During the summer of 1999, Usher played basketball at

'N Sync's Challenge for the Children benefit game at Georgia State University. The game raised money for different children's charities. Usher was joined on the court by Mase, Kobe Bryant, and all the guys from 'N Sync.

In Atlanta, Usher spends time with kids at local Boys & Girls Clubs. Usher supports the organization because it used to provide him with a place to go after school. "Every chance I get, I sit down with the kids and talk to them," he told the Associated Press. "I tell them, 'Do what you've got to do to succeed. I'm always going to encourage you.' " Usher's commitment to helping others is an inspiration to his many fans.

NOT JUST TALK

Usher doesn't just talk about making a difference. His actions speak as loudly as his words. In January 2000, Usher was driving near Atlanta and came upon a car accident.

The female driver of the car was escaping from the wreck, but her clothing was on fire. Usher immediately stopped at the scene and used his jacket to smother the flames. Usher stayed with the burned woman until the ambulance arrived. Sadly, the woman died from her terrible injuries a few weeks later. Her son was grateful, though, and called a radio station to thank Usher publicly for his brave actions.

USHER'S FUTURE

Usher's life has been so busy that he has not had much time for dating or relationships. The biggest loves in Usher's life are acting and music.

In 1999, Usher recorded a duet with Mariah Carey, the biggest-selling artist of the 1990s. Their song "How Much" is featured on her hit album *Rainbow*. His live album and video *Usher Live* was released in March 1999. They were recorded during a free concert that Usher performed in his childhood town of Chattanooga, Tennessee.

In March 2000, Usher went to Toronto to film the season opener of the Disney Channel series, "The Famous Jett Jackson." In the show, Usher played Zander Hall, an evil skateboarder and computer hacker.

With all the acting jobs, it's hard to believe that Usher has any time to record new music. Yet he will record a new album with Jermaine Dupri, the producer who helped *My Way* become such a huge success. Usher will write a lot of the new material, too.

It's obvious that Usher is a talented musician, actor, and performer with a bright future ahead of him. Usher told *Rolling Stone*: "My goal is to be successful and to change music and make a difference." Usher's fans know that he has been succeeding. He definitely will be around a long, long time!

Usher dresses for success.

TIMELINE

1978   •Usher Raymond IV was born in Dallas, Texas.

1980   •Usher and his mother move to Chattanooga, Tennessee, and she remarries.

1990   •Usher and his family move to Atlanta, Georgia.

1992   •Usher auditions for LaFace Records.

1993   •Usher performs on "Star Search" and wins Best Teen Male Vocalist.
•"Call Me A Mack," from the soundtrack for *Poetic Justice*, is released as Usher's first single.

1994   •The album *Usher* is released in August.
•"Think of You" hits the top ten.
•"U Will Know" is featured on the soundtrack for *Jason's Lyric*.

1995   •Usher records "Let's Straighten It Out" with Monica.

TIMELINE

1995
- Usher records a holiday jingle for Coca-Cola.

1996
- Usher graduates from high school.
- Usher contributes a song to the tribute album for the 1996 Olympics.

1997
- *My Way*, Usher's second album, is released.
- The single "You Make Me Wanna. . " sells more than one million copies.
- Usher is an opening performer on Puff Daddy's No Way Out tour.
- Usher appears on the TV show "Moesha."

1998
- Usher is named Billboard Entertainer of the Year.
- Usher is nominated for a Grammy Award for Best Male R&B Performance.
- Usher tours with Janet Jackson.
- In June, Usher appears in eight episodes of "The Bold and the Beautiful."

TIMELINE

1999   •The NAACP gives Usher an Image
         Award for Outstanding Actor in a
         Daytime Drama Series.
       •Usher appears in *She's All That*.
       •Usher costars with Vanessa Williams
         in *Light It Up*.
       •*Texas Rangers* begins filming.
       •*Usher Live* is released in March.

2000   •"The Famous Jett Jackson" is
         filmed in March.
       •The TV musical "Gepetto" airs.

FACT SHEET

Name	Usher Terry Raymond IV
Born	October 14, 1978
Birthplace	Dallas, Texas
Hometown	Atlanta, Georgia
Sign	Libra
Family	Jonetta Patton (J-Pat), mother; Usher Raymond III, father; James, half-brother
Hair/Eyes	Brown/Brown
Pets	Star and My King, both pitbulls
Car	Black Porsche Boxster

Favorites

Color	Yellow
Subjects	Music, Science
Singers	Michael Jackson, Marvin Gaye, Sammy Davis Jr., Stevie Wonder
Rapper	The Notorious B.I.G.

audition a try-out performance

ballad a slow song

chart a listing that ranks music sales

choreography dance moves

costar a person who stars in a film or TV show alongside another star

drama a serious television show

duet a song sung by two performers

gold record certificate awarded to a record that sells half a million (500,000) copies

Grammy Award an award given in recognition of musical achievement

mentor a trusted person who advises and guides someone

musical a show with music, singing, and dancing

nomination the selection of someone to be considered for an award

NEW WORDS

platinum record a certificate awarded to a record that sells one million copies

pop relating to popular music

producer the person who supervises the production of a record, film, or television program

puberty when a person's body is developing into adulthood

R&B rhythm and blues; music that includes elements of blues and African-American folk music

record label a company that produces and sells records

science fiction kind of story that deals with scientific subjects or alien beings

soundtrack the music recorded for a movie

spokesperson someone who is chosen to speak or represent an organization

FOR FURTHER READING

Laslo, Cynthia. *Brandy*. Danbury, CT: Children's Press, 2000.

Malkin, Mark S. *Usher: The Ultimate Entertainer*. Kansas City, MO: Andrews & McMeel, 1998.

Waggett, Gerald J. *Soap Opera Encyclopedia*. New York: HarperCollins Publishers, 1997.

RESOURCES

Arista Records: Usher
www.aristarec.com
This is the official site of Arista records. It contains an Usher biography and lots of pictures. Here you can download audio and video clips of Usher's music and find out about tour information.

Rock On The Net: Usher
www.rockonthenet.com/artists-u/usher main.htm
This site contains a biography, discography, and timeline of Usher's career. It also includes links to other Usher Web sites, as well as a database of information about other celebrities.

Usher: Peeps Republic Music News
www.peeps.com/usher/index.html
This site lets you download videos, songs, an interview, and shout-outs from Usher. It also contains great pictures and an extensive biography.

INDEX

ABOUT THE AUTHOR

Morgan Talmadge is a freelance writer and soccer coach living in Mt. Vernon, Iowa.